R. C. SCRIVEN

The *Prospect* of Whitby

ILLUSTRATED BY

Doreen Roberts

London

OXFORD UNIVERSITY PRESS

1971

Oxford University Press, Ely House, London W. 1

GLASGOW NEW YORK TORONTO MELBOURNE WELLINGTON
CAPE TOWN SALISBURY IBADAN NAIROBI DAR ES SALAAM LUSAKA ADDIS ABABA
BOMBAY CALCUTTA MADRAS KARACHI LAHORE DACCA
KUALA LUMPUR SINGAPORE HONG KONG TOKYO

© Oxford University Press 1971
First published 1965
First published in this edition 1971
ISBN 0 19 276040 8

Printed in Austria

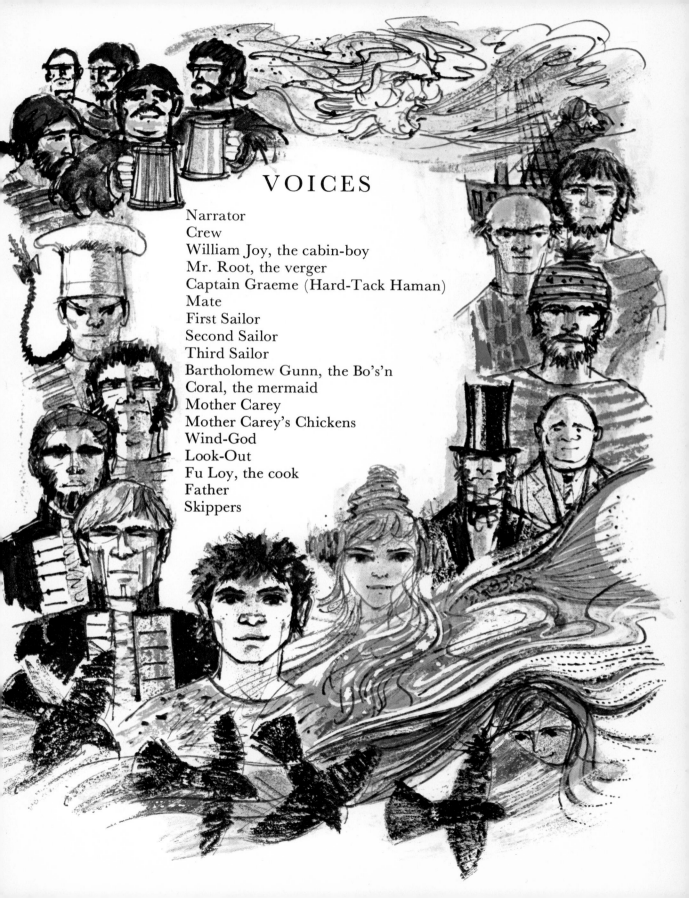

VOICES

Narrator
Crew
William Joy, the cabin-boy
Mr. Root, the verger
Captain Graeme (Hard-Tack Haman)
Mate
First Sailor
Second Sailor
Third Sailor
Bartholomew Gunn, the Bo's'n
Coral, the mermaid
Mother Carey
Mother Carey's Chickens
Wind-God
Look-Out
Fu Loy, the cook
Father
Skippers

NARRATOR: The *Prospect* was a Whitby ship,
a clipper tall and stately.
Her master's name was Captain Graeme,
a gaunt and grim and grey man.
The Seven Seas, so wide his fame,
all called him Hard-Tack Haman.

6

The Whitby men as hard as nails
who set her course and trimmed her sails
and took her helm in howling gales:
her hardy crew, as seamen do,
they cursed and loved her greatly.

NARRATOR: A hornpipe, a hornpipe, a hornpipe with heel-and-toe!
(continued)

CREW: When she returned to Whitby, O,
we danced it most ornately!

NARRATOR: Shore leave is sweet.

CREW: But all too fleet.
A week goes by like one day.

NARRATOR: The *Prospect*, she must go to sea
on the morning tide of Monday.
So William Joy, her cabin-boy,
sang in the choir on Sunday.

8

WILLIAM: *Safe from the perils on the sea,*
safe is our ship and so are we.

CREW: *For our landfall homecoming*
humble thanks to Thee we sing,
O Lord most high.

NARRATOR: Coral the mermaid, out in the bay,
combing the kinks from her silken locks,
heard their singing from far away.
She laid aside on the sea-wet rocks
her silver mirror, her golden comb,
and swam ashore through the spindrift foam
where North Sea horses neigh.

Making the foreshore's steep ascent
into church the mermaid went
silver-glittering from the beach—
ah! not to hear the preacher preach.
Demurely from a corner pew
she watched with eyes wave-green, sea-blue,
and in her heart a strange new joy—
William, the cabin-boy.

10

WILLIAM: *Holy, holy, holy,*
             Lord God of Hosts.

CREW: *Sea and land belong to Thee,*
             life and death, and so do we.

WILLIAM: *O Lord most high.*

NARRATOR: The service ended, one and all
             filed from pew and choir stall,
             but in silence prim and sly
             passed the little mermaid by.
             William, as taciturn as they,
             looked at her and glanced away.
             The verger, kindly Mr. Root,
             spared one word for Coral:

ROOT: Oot!

NARRATOR: Townsfolk saw the *Prospect* glide
              seaward on the morning tide.
              Watchers on the Abbey hill
              saw her royals spread and fill:
              the open sea they saw her make.
              Only a coastguard chanced to spy
              through the glass he clapped to his one good eye
              a mermaid swimming in her wake.

CREW: Hornpipe, a hornpipe, a hornpipe with heel-and-toe!
              A hornpipe . . .

12

GRAEME: Shiver my timbers! Avast, there, Mr. Mate!

MATE: Aye, aye, sir.

GRAEME: Give 'em the rope's end—
from now to the River Plate!

NARRATOR: Through the Channel and Westward, ho!
the crew were hazed with cuff and blow.
The mate by day and the skipper by night
kept the discipline fast and tight.
Watch by cruel watch, the two
knocked six bells out of the *Prospect*'s crew.
The men, including the cook Fu Loy,
knocked seven out of the cabin-boy.

NARRATOR: The wholesome diet was somewhat coarse.
(continued) One day hard tack, the next, salt horse.

FIRST SAILOR: Hard tack, hard tack.

SECOND SAILOR: Twice baked, twice black.

THIRD SAILOR: The captain sits him down to dine on chicken.

FIRST SAILOR: And Madeira wine.
What d'ye call it?

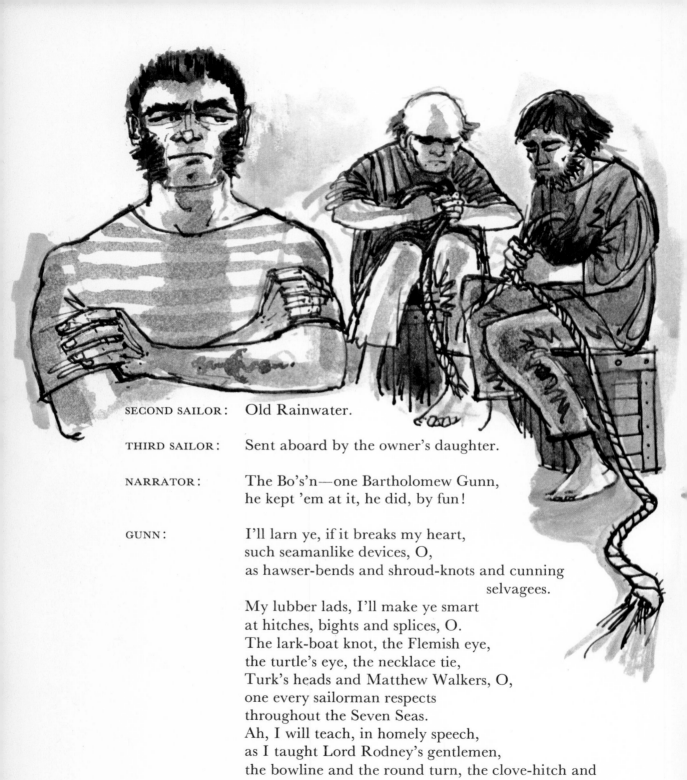

SECOND SAILOR: Old Rainwater.

THIRD SAILOR: Sent aboard by the owner's daughter.

NARRATOR: The Bo's'n—one Bartholomew Gunn,
he kept 'em at it, he did, by fun!

GUNN: I'll larn ye, if it breaks my heart,
such seamanlike devices, O,
as hawser-bends and shroud-knots and cunning
selvagees.
My lubber lads, I'll make ye smart
at hitches, bights and splices, O.
The lark-boat knot, the Flemish eye,
the turtle's eye, the necklace tie,
Turk's heads and Matthew Walkers, O,
one every sailorman respects
throughout the Seven Seas.
Ah, I will teach, in homely speech,
as I taught Lord Rodney's gentlemen,
the bowline and the round turn, the clove-hitch and
the reef,

16

NARRATOR: (The cabin-boy began to cry.)

GUNN: the frog, the toggled sheet bend,
             and you shall tie the tomfool knot
             to your p'ticular grief.

WILLIAM: Two bells in the middle watch.
             Why did I sign for cabin-boy?

CORAL: Ahoy, there! Ahoy, there!
             Dear William, ahoy!

WILLIAM: My ears, they do deceive me.

CORAL: Believe me, oh believe me,
my dearest William Joy.
I can tie the wind-knot, the wind-knot,
I can tie the wind-knot, the Lapland
                               witches use
and give their sailor sweethearts,
the Twelve Winds to unloose!
A knot far older than Stonehenge.
A knot that has no match.
Oh, you shall have a sweet revenge
on all your messmates!
Catch!

WILLIAM: Thanks.

CORAL: William, sweet William,
my love's tied in the wind-knot. The very best of luck.
But do not loose the wind-knot, the wind-knot,
do not loose the wind-knot until eight bells have struck.

(Eight bells strike, and the sinister sound of rising wind is
heard far off.)

18

FIRST SAILOR:	Deck, ahoy!
GRAEME:	Aye, aye, look-out?
FIRST SAILOR:	The sun's blood-red this morning.
GRAEME:	Mr. Mate!
MATE:	Aye, aye, sir.
GRAEME:	Hard a-starboard!
CREW:	Messmates: the sailors' warning!
WILLIAM:	The sky's a crimson lake!
FIRST SAILOR:	The royals back!
SECOND SAILOR:	The stuns'ls shake!
GRAEME:	All hands on deck! I'll take the wheel.

NARRATOR: The *Prospect* shuddered to her keel.
             Out of the North-East rose the gale
             and struck her masts like a whirling flail.
             Her three masts groaned, her ensign shredded.
             Her bowsprit bucked and South she headed.
             With a bone in her teeth she gripped the bolder
             in the flying spume when the rollers rolled her.

             But Hard-Tack Haman's voice was dry:

GRAEME: No other ship is like her
             when Mother Carey's chickens fly
             before her dolphin-striker.

CHICKENS: Mother Carey's a-calling.

MOTHER CAREY: Ai-eee!

20

CHICKENS: Disaster's forerunners are we.
Our wings are as dark as the sea
as they skim through the flecks of the foam.
The wind-god is shouting aloud.

WIND-GOD: I will humble the tall and the proud!

CHICKENS: The spindrift shall weave her a shroud:
Mother Carey is calling us home.

MOTHER CAREY: Ai-eee! Ai-eeeee! Ai-eeeeeee!

NARRATOR: But the crew all knew, by Haman's grin,
that never a stitch would *he* take in.

GRAEME: Lash me to the wheel. By thunder!
I'll round the Horn or drive her under.

CORAL: My love, unloose the wind-knot,
the wind-knot:
let out another strand.

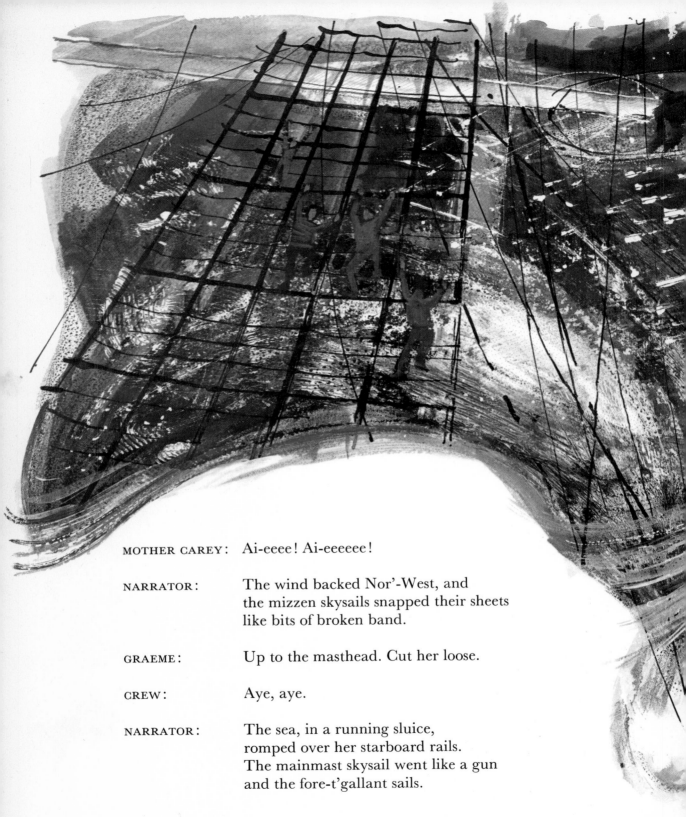

MOTHER CAREY: Ai-eeee! Ai-eeeeee!

NARRATOR: The wind backed Nor'-West, and
the mizzen skysails snapped their sheets
like bits of broken band.

GRAEME: Up to the masthead. Cut her loose.

CREW: Aye, aye.

NARRATOR: The sea, in a running sluice,
romped over her starboard rails.
The mainmast skysail went like a gun
and the fore-t'gallant sails.

22

GRAEME: Into the rigging!

NARRATOR: Along the yard they clawed like cats
             to furl and reef and cut.
             But lo! The Norther whirled the snow
             which made them blind as bats.
             Their hands forgot the proper knot,
             sure though they were of foot.
             Five hurtled from the yard-arm, the yard-arm,
             into the sea below.

BO'S'N: As I am a bo's'n, a bo's'n,
             their mother wits were froz'n
             such tomfool knots to tie.

23

CORAL: My love, re-knot the wind-knot, the wind-knot,
with all your might and main.

NARRATOR: So William tied it tight.
The sea went down. The wind fell light.

The wind-god slewed his mouth about,
North-about and South-about,
The skipper felt his senses reel.

GRAEME: She will not answer to the wheel.

NARRATOR: Fore, main and mizzen sails fell slack.
He tried to veer. He tried to tack.
The skipper's face grew leaner, lanker.

GRAEME: Set jib and flying jib and spanker!

CREW: Aye, aye.

NARRATOR: As seamen do when all else fails,
he tried to steer her by her sails.

CORAL: My love, shake loose the wind-knot's tangle.

NARRATOR: And now from this, then from that angle,
the wind, obedient perforce,
blew back the *Prospect* on her course.
Vainly Hard-Tack Haman raged.

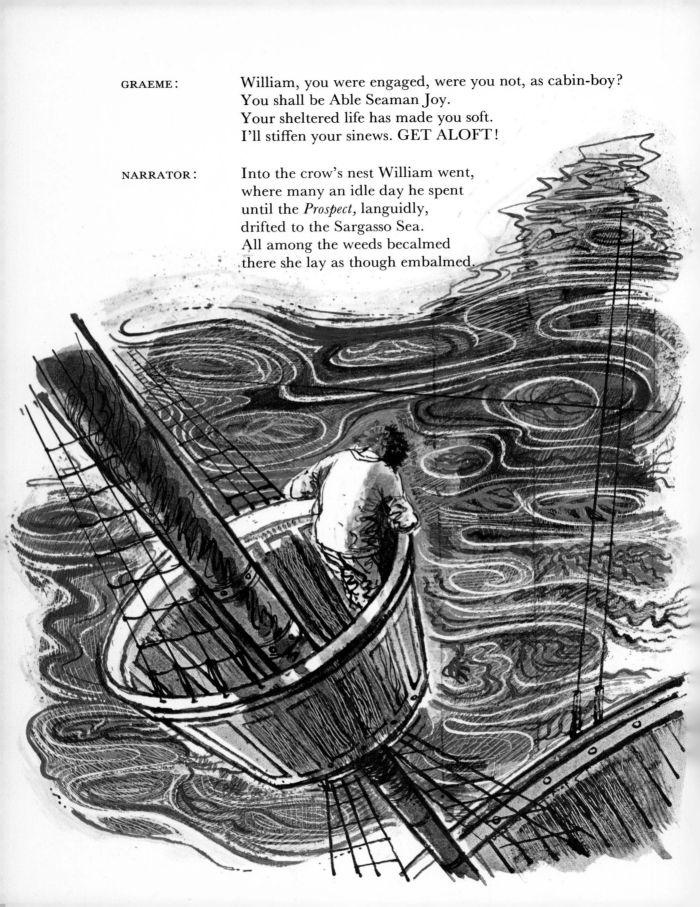

GRAEME: William, you were engaged, were you not, as cabin-boy?
You shall be Able Seaman Joy.
Your sheltered life has made you soft.
I'll stiffen your sinews. GET ALOFT!

NARRATOR: Into the crow's nest William went,
where many an idle day he spent
until the *Prospect,* languidly,
drifted to the Sargasso Sea.
All among the weeds becalmed
there she lay as though embalmed.

GRAEME:	Bo's'n.
BO'S'N:	Aye, aye, sir.
GRAEME:	Make and mend.
BO'S'N:	I'll make 'em skip with my rope's end. You shabby, shoddy shellbacks, you: out with your tackle and set-to. You shall sew and sew like fun as I'm Bartholomew, son of a Gunn.

CORAL: My love, my love: the wind-knot.

NARRATOR: Ho! With a sudden snort
              the wind-god lunged from the West and plunged
              the startled ship to port.

BO'S'N: Save me!

NARRATOR: Before one stitch was stitched
              into the sea the bo's'n pitched.
              The long weeds got, the strong weeds got,
              a grip on arm and thigh.
              They fastened his thumbs with a lark-boat knot,
              his toes with a necklace tie.
              In a running bowline on a bight
              they lashed his wrists and ankles tight.
              They wound about and bound about
              and reefed his bo's'n's coat,
              and down he went in the weed-green sea
              with a shroud-knot at his throat.

28

CORAL: My love, re-tie the wind-knot.

NARRATOR: And down the wind went, too.

GRAEME: The ship must have a Jonah.
I'll smell him out, by heck!
Jump to it there, my hearties,
and holystone the deck.
Scrub, scrub. See to it, Bo's'n Joy.

NARRATOR: Promotion, so I've heard it said,
sometimes goes to a good man's head.
Now William held the rope's end,
he hastened to employ.
An act which made the jealous mate
a painful sight to contemplate.

MATE: A Jonah, eh? The Old Man's right.
Bo's'n. Belay, belay.
What knot is that you clutch so tight?
Give it to me I say.

WILLIAM: Let go! Let go!

MATE: A word and a blow
is all you'll get from me.

CORAL: Look out, my love!

MATE: A mermaid!

NARRATOR: The wind-knot slipped. The *Prospect* dipped
her bowsprit savagely.
And as they strove, the Sou'-West clove
a path through the weed-choked sea.
A curled wave's weight
struck down the mate,
and overboard went he.

But William leapt to the wheel and kept
the wind-knot in his hand.
Through every shroud the storm shrieked loud,
which made his soul rejoice.

GRAEME: Right, Mr. Mate. Just keep her straight.

NARRATOR: Rang Hard-Tack Haman's voice.
A mate! A mate! On, on, elate,
our William steered his ship.
Not till three bells in the forenoon watch
did he relax his grip,
for to re-tie the wind-knot with one hand and his teeth.
Salt caked her in a sheath.
But the *Prospect* sailed under a blue, blue sky
with a bluer sea beneath.

NARRATOR:
(continued)

Before a breeze of pure heart's ease
swanlike she rippled now.
The look-out, he sang ringingly:

LOOK-OUT:

Islands! On either bow!

GRAEME:

Then I will dine. Madeira wine
and chicken-soup, Fu Loy!
Hard tack for the crew. Salt horse for you
with m'compliments, Mr. Joy.

NARRATOR:

With sighs the crew sat down to chew.

CORAL:

Sweet William! Ahoy!

WILLIAM:

Beg pardon, ma'am.

CORAL:

My love!

WILLIAM:

I am
no more a cabin-boy.

NARRATOR:

Fu Loy went hurrying by the rail,
and Coral, as he passed,
struck the blue water with her tail.

GRAEME: *This* chicken-soup? Avast!
You son of a sea-cook . . .

COOK: Please. No flog!

GRAEME: Flog? I'll maroon ye, you yellow dog!

NARRATOR: The *Prospect*'s log I hate to soil.
When Fu Loy landed with moil and toil
cannibals cooked him in boiling oil.

What cared Haman, that hardened sinner?

33

GRAEME: Hi, Mr. Mate! I want my dinner.
Fu Loy and you were far too pally.
You're cook now.

WILLIAM: But . . .

GRAEME: Get into that galley.

NARRATOR: In the first watch, when every spar
seemed to touch a tropic star,
Haman leaned on a capstan bar
and struck a match for his cigar,
watched from the water's starlit sheen
by Coral's eyes, sea-blue, wave-green.

Softly she called to William Joy.

CORAL: William! Now for your finest ploy.
Loose every tie in the wind-knot. Quick!

NARRATOR: The stars went out as with one flick.

MOTHER CAREY: Ai-eee! Ai-eeeeee!

CHICKENS: Mother Carey is calling. We come.

NARRATOR: Greek fire made the water burn.
                Each of the twelve winds struck in turn.
                The *Prospect*, to the hail's deep drum,
                spun widdershins like a tee-to-tum.
                The whirling capstan—

CREW: Glory be!

NARRATOR: —tossed Haman into the maelstrom sea.

                William tied the wind-knot, the wind-knot,
                and home he sailed the *Prospect*
                on the Trade Wind's steady lee.

CREW: Hornpipe, a hornpipe, a hornpipe with heel-and-toe.

NARRATOR: All Whitby made her welcome, O,
           upon the old stone quay.
           Martha, the owner's daughter, the foremost one was she.
           Deep, deep in love with William Joy—
           returned a man, not a cabin-boy—
           fell Martha instantly.

           And up and spake her father, O:

FATHER: Consenting full and free
you shall command the *Prospect*.

NARRATOR: The owner said, said he.

Cried William sturdily:

Cried William sturdily:

WILLIAM: I will!

NARRATOR: In the bleak church beneath the hill
              the banns were read and man and boy
              congratulated Captain Joy;
              and every skipper on shore leave
              drank with him on his wedding eve.

SKIPPERS: Red sky at night is our delight,
              at sunrise, sailors' warning.

38

WILLIAM: Rise soon, rise soon! The young May moon
holds back my bride's adorning.
Drink deep, messmates, for the *Prospect* waits
for the knot to be tied in the morning.

NARRATOR: Coral, the mermaid, out in the bay,
heard their singing afar, afar.
Her comb, her mirror, she cast away
and swam ashore with her sea-guitar.

Of *bêche-de-mer* was its sound-box made
in gold and mother-of-pearl inlaid.
And over its strings her fingers strayed.

CORAL: The moon has trailed her shimmering cloak
as delicate as gossamer
in black and silver filigree
across the rippling waves.
But mortal eyes have never seen
the moonlight's sea-refracted stir
in shifting, magic fantasy
through my enchanted caves.

But stranger than the moon's cold spell
are the fierce hearts of men to me.
Because they fear the cruel sea
they dare her in their ships.
I, too, have charms to change the heart
of men. My love, come then to me.
By silver mirror, golden comb:
Come, sailor: seek my lips.

NARRATOR: The fiddles stopped their scraping
as William started up.

He tore at his necktie. He dashed down his cup.
Men crowded from the tavern. They stood bereft of speech.
They saw him in the moonlight go racing down the beach.
They saw him stumble through the foam
between the sea and land.

42

They did not see the wave that snatched the wind-knot
from his hand,
and toss it away across the bay
where the North Sea horses roam.
But they saw the *Prospect*'s riding lights
dim when the sea-fret came.
And they heard a high, wild cry
as he called her by her name.

WILLIAM: Coral!

CORAL: My love! My Joy!

NARRATOR: And that was the end of the captain
who rose from cabin-boy.

43

CREW: Hornpipe, a hornpipe, a hornpipe with heel-and-toe!
That's what they dance in Whitby, O,
captain or cabin-boy.